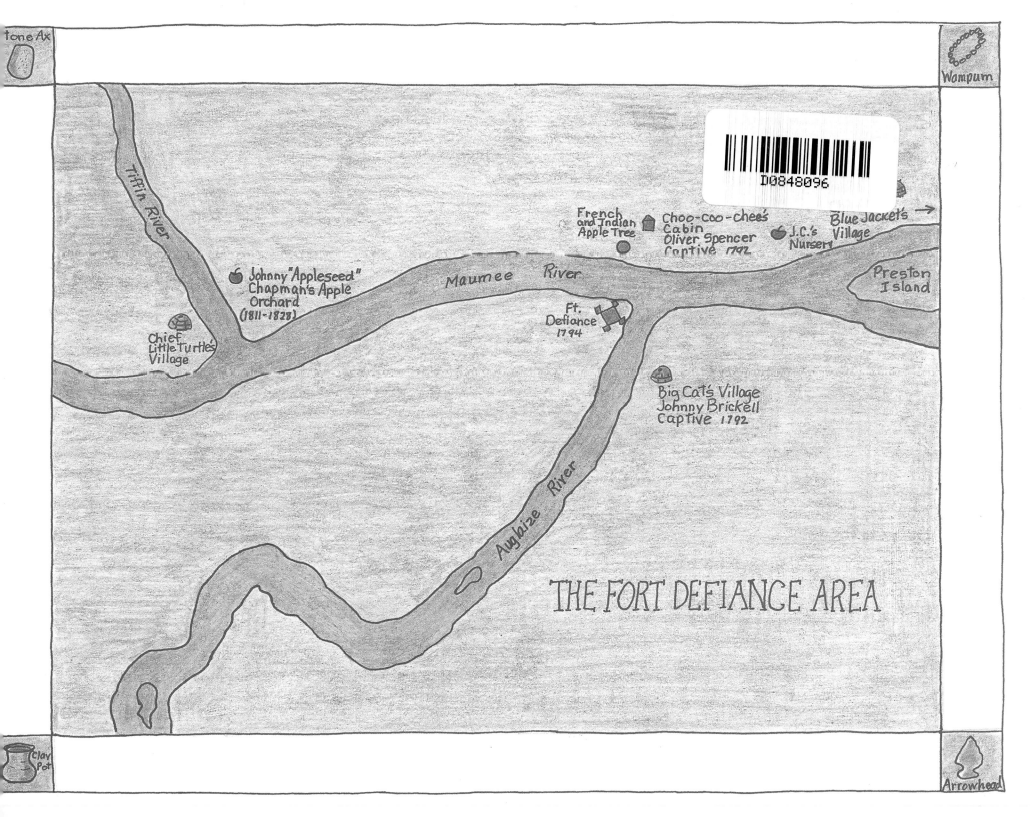

THE FORT DEFIANCE AREA

Hold The Fort

Hold The Fort

Story *and* Illustrations
by Sally Snyder

To the Hauesperger Family...
Hope you enjoy "Hold the Fort"!

Sally Snyder
— 2005 —

FALLEN TIMBERS PRESS
Defiance, Ohio

2nd Printing: 2004

ISBN: 1-882203-99-2
© Copyright 2003 Sally Snyder
All rights reserved

To order additional copies of *HOLD THE FORT* or to make arrangements for the author to come to your school, please call:
  Fallen Timbers Press
  1341 Ironwood Court
  Defiance, OH 43512
  419.782.0778
  www.holdthefort.org

Printed in Canada

Library of Congress Control Number: 2003092074

For my family and former students—

With special gratitude to Marcy Hawley and Orange Frazer Press
for their beautiful layout and design work and for
making my dream a reality.

As the great bald eagle soars high above northwest Ohio, its breath-taking view is like a patchwork quilt. Carefully planted fields of corn, wheat, oats, and beans can be seen for miles and miles across this beautiful, flat land. Just as the old quilts were made of layers of recycled fabric, this rich land is made up of layers of rock, soil, and winding rivers that have a fascinating story to tell.

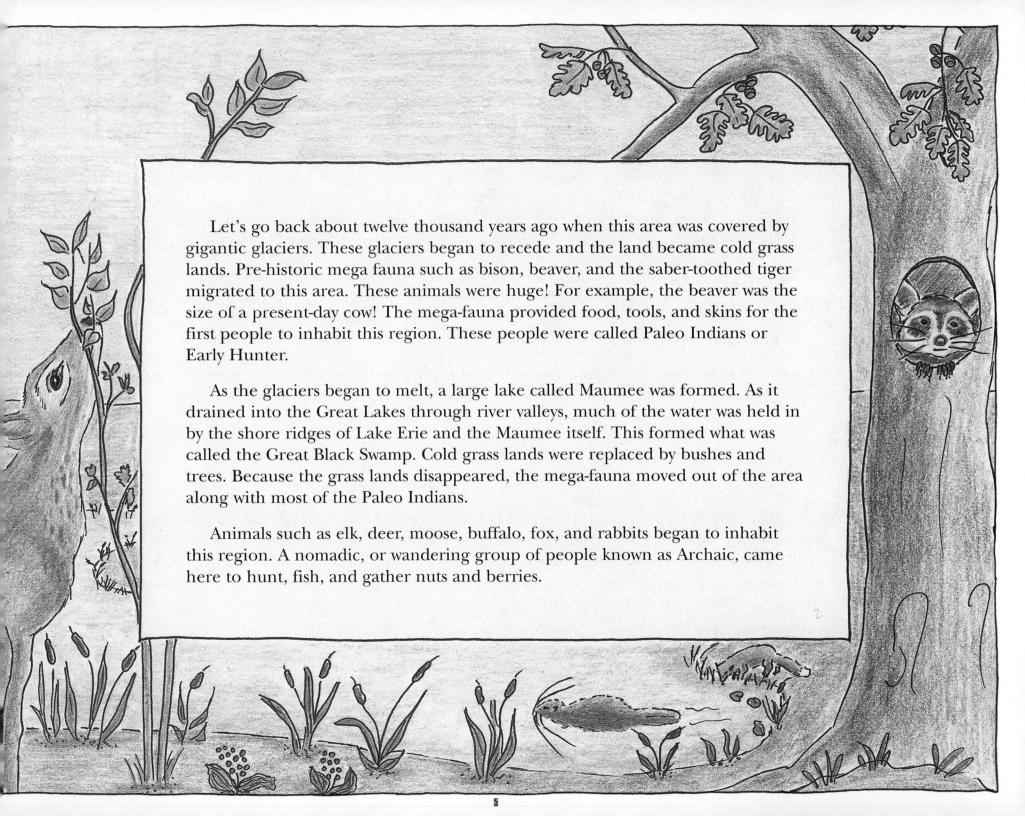

Let's go back about twelve thousand years ago when this area was covered by gigantic glaciers. These glaciers began to recede and the land became cold grass lands. Pre-historic mega fauna such as bison, beaver, and the saber-toothed tiger migrated to this area. These animals were huge! For example, the beaver was the size of a present-day cow! The mega-fauna provided food, tools, and skins for the first people to inhabit this region. These people were called Paleo Indians or Early Hunter.

As the glaciers began to melt, a large lake called Maumee was formed. As it drained into the Great Lakes through river valleys, much of the water was held in by the shore ridges of Lake Erie and the Maumee itself. This formed what was called the Great Black Swamp. Cold grass lands were replaced by bushes and trees. Because the grass lands disappeared, the mega-fauna moved out of the area along with most of the Paleo Indians.

Animals such as elk, deer, moose, buffalo, fox, and rabbits began to inhabit this region. A nomadic, or wandering group of people known as Archaic, came here to hunt, fish, and gather nuts and berries.

Teakettle

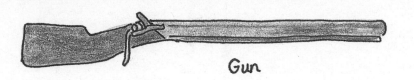
Gun

Jug

Pelt

Powder
Horn

By about one thousand B.C., the people inhabiting the Great Black Swamp began to change their way of life. They started to grow crops and make pottery. They also became more interested in death and burial ceremonies. In our region, these people were called Mound Builders. Archeologists have given them other names such as Adena, Hopewell, and Fort Ancient.

By the 1600's, the Native Americans living here belonged to the Algonquian or Iroquoian Leagues. Some of the tribes included in these leagues were the Delaware, Miami, Ottawa, Shawnee, Seneca, and Wyandot. They worked in their gardens, caught fish, hunted, and gathered berries.

The arrival of people from Europe brought about many changes for the Native Americans. French fur traders came to this area with items made from shiny metal. For example, they were bringing in knives, guns, and jewelry. The Indians were fascinated with the shiny metal objects and would gladly trade furs for them. The French traders preferred the beaver pelt. These pelts were sent to Europe to be made into fancy hats and coats.

The Native Americans of Ohio lived peacefully, trading with the French until about 1650. Iroquois hunters and trappers to the east had killed off most of the fur-bearing animals in their homeland. They wanted to continue their trade with the English, so they turned to the rich hunting grounds of Ohio. The Iroquois waged a war against the Indians living here. Some people were killed, while others fled. The Iroquois claimed the land and the fur trading business for themselves. They did not come here to live, simply to hunt deer and beaver. This period in Ohio history is referred to as the Beaver Wars. Due to these wars, no one lived here from about 1650 to 1700.

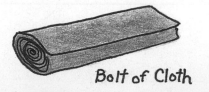
Bolt of Cloth

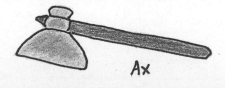
Ax

Metal
Bucket

By the 1730's there were many English settlements, or colonies, along the east coast. More and more Native Americans migrated to this area. Both French and British fur traders and explorers worked hard to make friends with the Indians.

Tensions grew as France and England wanted to claim this land for their countries. This tension lead to the outbreak of the French and Indian War. (1754-1763) Most of the Indians fought with the French. Though it was very difficult for the British, they did win the war. They were given Canada and all of the land east of the Mississippi River. Both France and England signed a treaty, or agreement, in 1763. Most of the French left Ohio.

Ottawa Chief Pontiac

An Ottawa Chief named Pontiac had fought with the French in the French and Indian War. It angered him to see the British moving into this territory, cutting down trees and building homes.

In the spring of 1763, Pontiac organized his tribe and allies from the Wyandot, Potawotomi, Miami, Delaware, Seneca, Shawnee and other tribes to get rid of the British. They would receive no help from the French. The tribes attacked all of the British forts. By late October, a huge British force was sent to attack the Indians. Pontiac had to face the fact that the British were here to stay. He and his people surrendered. (Historians believe that he was born near the confluence of the Maumee and Auglaize Rivers in the early 1700's.)

Even though the French and Indian War had ended, the British rulers decided to send ten thousand soldiers called "redcoats" across the ocean to the colonies. King George III had become the British ruler and wanted to "keep an eye on his children" in America. The British Parliament, or lawmakers, passed the Quartering Act, which said that the American colonists had to pay for the redcoats' quarters, or living space. They also had to give the soldiers candles, fuel, salt and bedding. This made the Americans very angry!

England continued to find other ways to tax the colonists. This caused them to rebel. England sent even more troops to America! Then on April 19, 1775 British soldiers and a group of colonists fired at each other in Lexington, Massachusetts. No one knows who fired the first shot! The American Revolutionary War had begun!

The war became official when the Declaration of Independence was signed by our country's leaders on July 4, 1776. Written by Thomas Jefferson, the Declaration stated that America would be willing to fight for its independence from England. There was great excitement when the colonists heard the news! Like our July 4 celebrations today, firecrackers were set off, bells rang, and there was dancing in the streets!

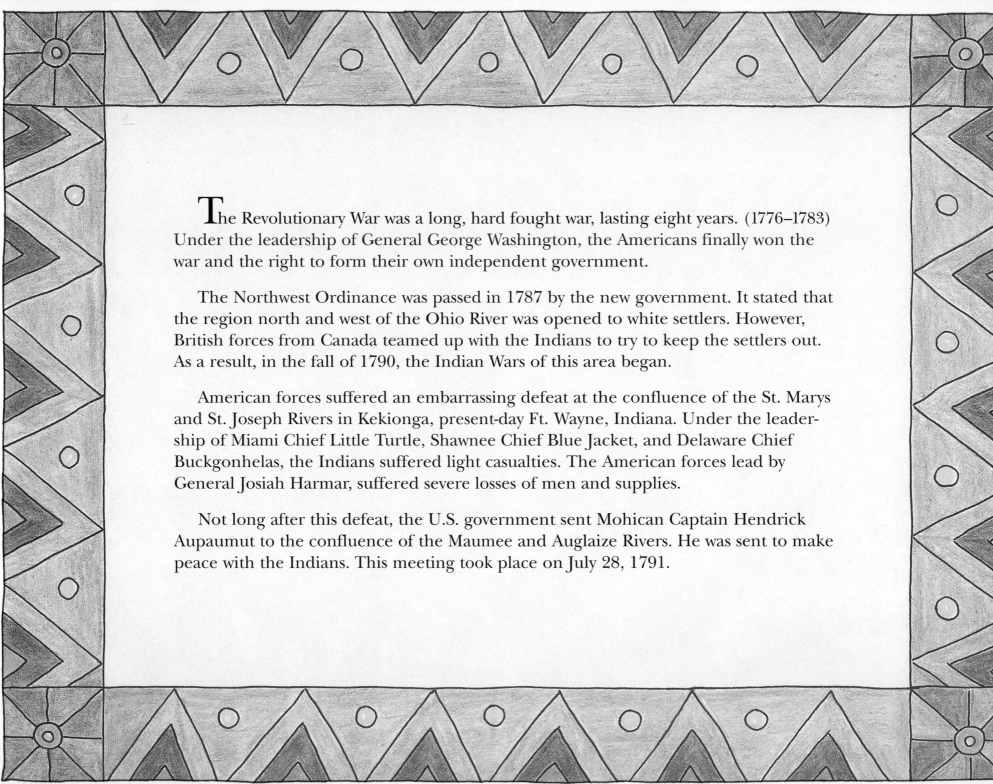

The Revolutionary War was a long, hard fought war, lasting eight years. (1776–1783) Under the leadership of General George Washington, the Americans finally won the war and the right to form their own independent government.

The Northwest Ordinance was passed in 1787 by the new government. It stated that the region north and west of the Ohio River was opened to white settlers. However, British forces from Canada teamed up with the Indians to try to keep the settlers out. As a result, in the fall of 1790, the Indian Wars of this area began.

American forces suffered an embarrassing defeat at the confluence of the St. Marys and St. Joseph Rivers in Kekionga, present-day Ft. Wayne, Indiana. Under the leadership of Miami Chief Little Turtle, Shawnee Chief Blue Jacket, and Delaware Chief Buckgonhelas, the Indians suffered light casualties. The American forces lead by General Josiah Harmar, suffered severe losses of men and supplies.

Not long after this defeat, the U.S. government sent Mohican Captain Hendrick Aupaumut to the confluence of the Maumee and Auglaize Rivers. He was sent to make peace with the Indians. This meeting took place on July 28, 1791.

During this time, many Native Americans were living here. Indians from all over North America gathered for the meeting with Captain Aupaumut. During this council, they made it clear to the captain that they did not want white people coming to this area. They wanted all American troops and the people north of the Ohio River removed. There was no peace settlement!

In November 1791, there was another major campaign against the Indians in the Maumee Valley near present-day Ft. Recovery, Ohio. It was lead by General Arthur St. Clair. His forces were soundly defeated by the Indians under the leadership of Little Turtle, Blue Jacket, and Buckgonhelas. The Indians returned to their villages along the rivers feeling confident that the Americans would not bother them again. How wrong they were!

President
George Washington

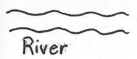
River

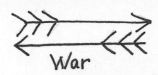
War

Sun

Star

General
Anthony Wayne

Moon

President George Washington had to find a leader that could win control over the Indians, so settlers could move into northwest Ohio. The attacks of Generals' Harmar and St. Clair made the Indians even more determined. Therefore, President Washington's choice for a General to lead the United States Army had to be someone with outstanding leadership abilities. During the American Revolution there was a man who had shown these very qualities. This person was none other than Major General Anthony Wayne. In April 1792, President Washington appointed General Wayne to train and lead the army.

Good

Peace

Bad

Moccasins

Hoop and Pole

That summer, a young boy by the name of Oliver Spencer and his family had gone to Cincinnati to visit friends. When they arrived, his mother and sister wanted to shop. His father wanted to talk farm business with men at the mill. Oliver became bored! He wanted to go home! After thinking it over, he decided to show them…he would go home by himself! Oliver started his dangerous journey down the river and found himself involved in an adventure he had never bargained for!

Two young warriors appeared out of the wilderness and captured Oliver! He nearly lost his life trying to escape. They brought him north from the Cincinnati area to the confluence. He was taken to White Loon, the son of a Mohawk Chief, who then turned him over to his mother, Cooh-coo-chee. Her little cabin was nestled on a hill near the Maumee River, the present-day site of Pontiac Park. Cooh-coo-chee was saddened by the death of her husband and her son thought a young boy would bring her joy.

Oliver learned the Native American ways quickly. He was taught how to hunt with a bow and arrow, gather wood, carry water for cooking and other chores. He enjoyed Native American songs and dances and learned to speak their language.

Even though Oliver received excellent care, he became very homesick. Therefore, white traders and government officials, including President Washington, worked out a plan for his return home. However, it would take two years before he would be reunited with his family. Leaving the Black Swamp, the travelers went to Detroit and then east to Niagara Falls. Next, they went south to Pittsburgh. From there they traveled the great Ohio River back to Cincinnati. Perhaps they chose this route since the Indian Wars were raging across Ohio.

Corn Husk Doll

Basket and Dice Game

Oliver Spencer grew into a fine young man, becoming a minister and writer. It is through his writings and those of other captives that we have a better picture of "the glaize," as the Defiance area was called in the early days. He tells of bustling Indian villages along the Maumee and Auglaize Rivers. For example, closest to the confluence was the Delaware village lead by Big Cat. He was part of Chief Buckgonhelas' council. Johnny Brickell, another brave, young captive, lived in this village.

Johnny was born near Pittsburgh, Pennsylvania. In 1791, at the age of about ten, he was captured by the Delaware Indians. Johnny was severely mistreated by his captors. At one point, he almost died.

After making several stops along the way, Johnny and his captors settled on the Maumee River at the Glaize. He was turned over to Big Cat and it was at this point that life began to change for him. Big Cat helped Johnny become an expert hunter. They lived by the river in the summer, catching fish and growing corn. In the winter, they would go on long hunting trips around the Scioto River. Johnny enjoyed learning the Native American customs.

In his writings, Oliver Spencer also mentioned a village at the mouth of the Tiffin River. This is where Chief Little Turtle and his Miami people lived. Blue Jacket's Shawnee village was located on the north side of the Maumee River, about one mile east of the confluence.

As the Indian Wars continued, the Native Americans were divided on their next course of action. Some nations were in favor of giving up their land to the American settlers. Others wanted to fight for what they felt belonged to them. In September 1792, a grand council was held at the Glaize. One of the largest gatherings of Native Americans to be held in this country, took place right here! There were about four thousand Indians with many nations represented. After many days of debate, they decided they would be willing to meet with the U.S. government. This meeting was planned for the summer of 1793 and would take place on the Sandusky River.

However, Chief Little Turtle had other plans. He lead a raid into southern Ohio to show the United States that they did not want white settlements north of the Ohio River. Even though it was a successful raid, the Indians realized that the government had no intentions of keeping the settlers out of this area. Therefore, the meeting on the Sandusky River never took place.

Little Turtle, Blue Jacket, and Buckgonhelas agreed on a strategy. They would continue to attack small groups of whites on the Ohio River and destroy their supply lines, but would not attack the forts. They would also continue to count on the British for supplies.

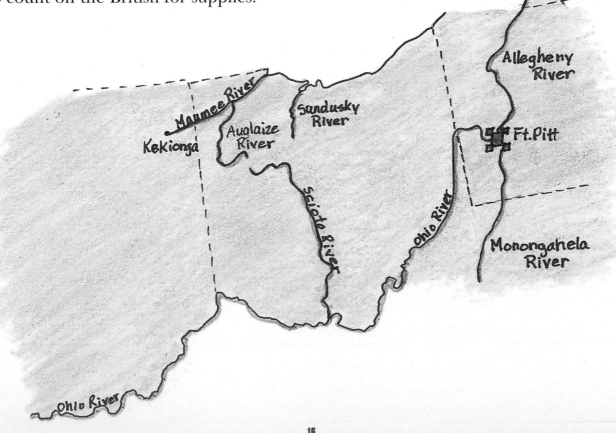

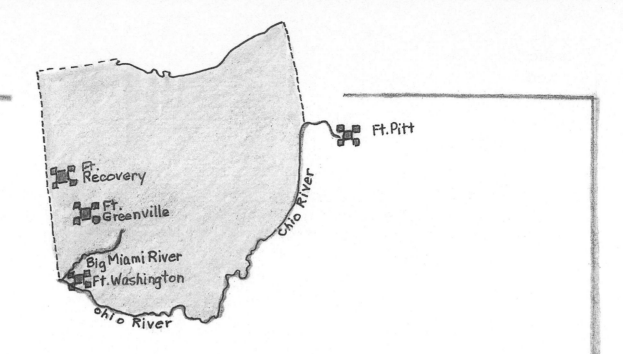

General Wayne had begun to train his forces at Pittsburgh in the spring of 1792. On October 7, 1793, after several encampments, they moved to the southwest branch of the Big Miami River. By October 13, they halted at the future site of Fort Greenville.

During the spring and summer of 1794, over fifteen hundred warriors came to the confluence preparing to fight the white man. All whites living in the area were forced to fight with the Indians. They began to move south on the 19th and 20th of June, attacking supply lines and outposts.

Late in December, General Wayne decided to build another fort further north to serve as an outpost for his scouts. It would also send a message of defiance to the Indians. The fort would be constructed near the site of the earlier defeat of St. Clair. He first thought of calling it Fort Defiance, but decided to name it Fort Recovery. The fort was built in four days and became the center of Wayne's scouting expeditions.

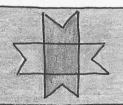

General Wayne was planning a winter attack at the confluence. He knew he would be able to move his well-trained army across the frozen swamp. However, in January, a small group of Delaware Indians from the confluence came to him to speak of peace. Wayne warmly received the representatives. The general's supplies were low and many of his soldiers were sick. Wayne and the Indians came to an agreement. There would be a peace conference and all white prisoners would be returned. There would be no more raids and they would be in contact for further negotiations by February 14. General Wayne ordered his troops not to attack any Indians unless they appeared to be dangerous.

This act of peace on the part of the Delaware Indians brought British spokesman, Matthew Elliot, to the confluence to speak with them. The Indians held another council meeting to discuss General Wayne's offer to have a major conference in February. Elliot persuaded them not to hold a peace conference with the general.

As a result, on the evening of June 29, 1794, a group of two thousand Indians attacked a supply convoy on its way to Fort Recovery. They captured all of the horses, killed several men, and attacked the fort. A band of Indians from the Great Lakes region was not following Little Turtle's plan. This band of Indians left the battlegrounds and returned to the confluence. Within a short time, they returned to their homes in Mackinac.

Chief Little Turtle was angered by the lack of obedience to his leadership. He said he would not lead his people unless he could have complete control of the Indian forces, and a cannon supplied by the British along with twenty British soldiers to fire it. The British refusal to supply the cannon and the fact that Indian forces were down to eight hundred, lead to a major decision. The great Chief Little Turtle felt they should make peace with General Wayne, "the chief who never sleeps." The other Indians did not agree and Blue Jacket took over as war chief.

General Wayne felt he had no choice but to put his troops into the field and attack the Indians at the confluence. On August 2, 1794 he moved his force of thirty-five hundred men northward. They built Fort Adams on the St. Marys River. It was at this site that an event took place that could have completely changed the history of Defiance and northwest Ohio.

On the second day of construction of Fort Adams, General Wayne was resting in his tent. All of a sudden a huge tree fell on him, pinning him underneath! Fortunately, he was not killed. However, his leg was seriously injured. It was discovered that a tree stump had broken the fall of the tree and saved his life! This injury would make the days and months ahead very difficult for the general.

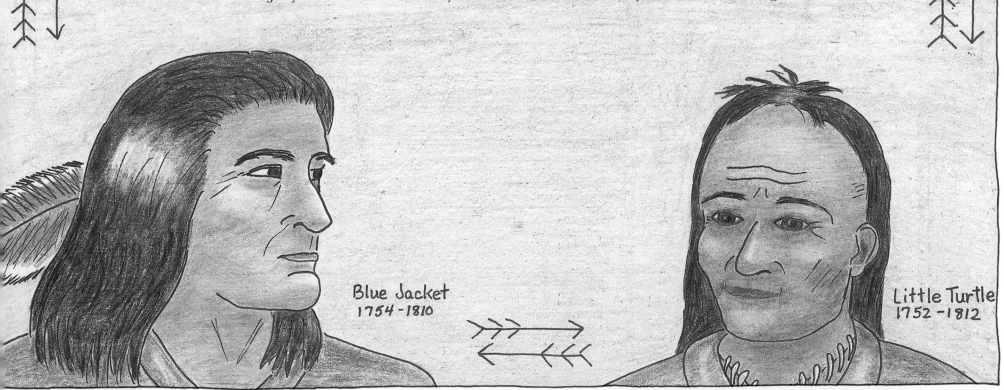

Blue Jacket
1754-1810

Little Turtle
1752-1812

General Wayne's army moved on toward the confluence. When they arrived on August 8, they found the Indian villages abandoned. The soldiers' journals described the scene as one of great beauty. It is at this spectacular site, where the Maumee and Auglaize Rivers meet, that General Wayne had his soldiers build his strongest fort of all. It took them eight days to build and was given the name Fort Defiance. What was once a Native American stronghold had been changed into a frontier outpost of the United States Army.

General Wayne sent a captured Indian up the river to offer peace with his people. If they wanted peace, the Indian was to return. He did not return. General Wayne tried a second time, but still there was no answer.

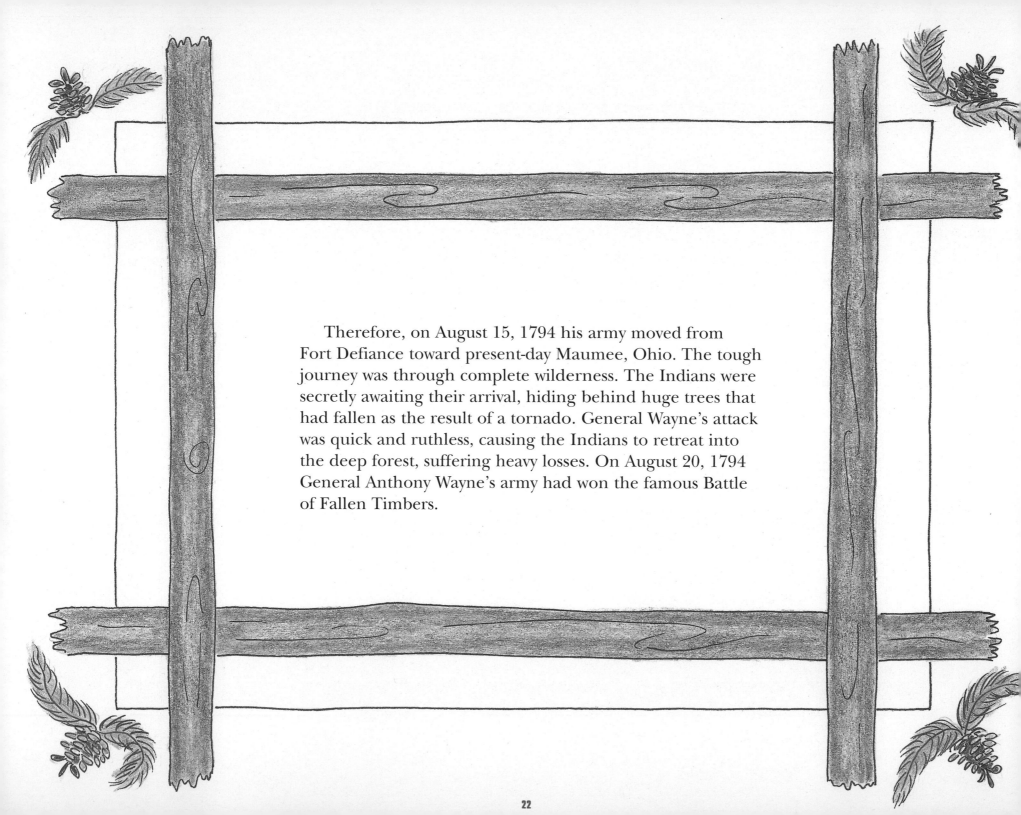

Therefore, on August 15, 1794 his army moved from Fort Defiance toward present-day Maumee, Ohio. The tough journey was through complete wilderness. The Indians were secretly awaiting their arrival, hiding behind huge trees that had fallen as the result of a tornado. General Wayne's attack was quick and ruthless, causing the Indians to retreat into the deep forest, suffering heavy losses. On August 20, 1794 General Anthony Wayne's army had won the famous Battle of Fallen Timbers.

Following the Battle of Fallen Timbers, General Wayne started the march back to Fort Defiance on August 23. It was thought that the British might join forces with the Indians and attack at the confluence. Wayne ordered his men to reinforce and improve the fort. This attack never took place and eventually General Wayne moved on to Kekionga to build Fort Wayne.

One year later, on August 3, 1795, the Treaty of Greenville was signed by the Indians. A section of this treaty made Fort Defiance one of three places where prisoners would be exchanged and another part set aside a six square mile reserve at the confluence for white settlers. Indians were allowed only to pass through or stop by to trade.

At about this same time, Johnny Brickell was given his freedom. It was very hard for him to leave his Native American family and friends. He eventually settled on the Scioto River near present-day Columbus, Ohio. It is believed that he was the first white, permanent settler in the Columbus area.

In March of 1796, just fifty-six soldiers remained at Fort Defiance. A trading post had been built nearby. There was little activity at the confluence in the late 1700's and early 1800's.

On March 1, 1803, a very important event took place. Ohio became the seventeenth state to join the union. Ohio proudly accepted its place as a member of the United States of America!

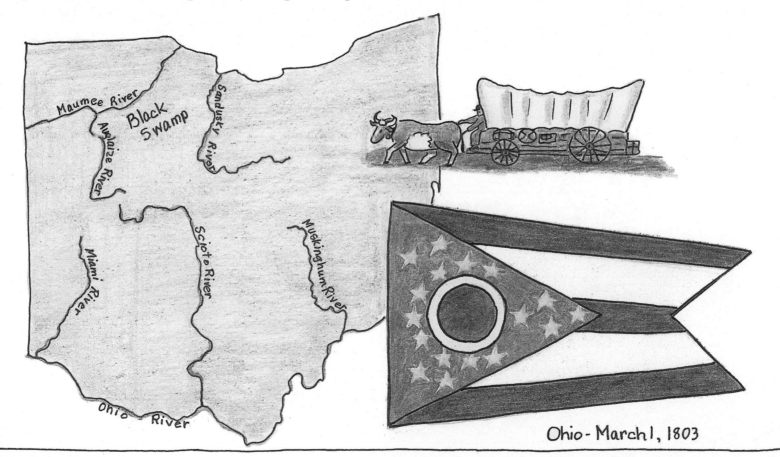

Ohio - March 1, 1803

In 1808 a large band of Shawnee Indians under the leadership of Tecumseh and his brother the Prophet, was ignoring the Treaty of Greenville that had brought the Indian Wars to a close. The British became involved by giving them supplies. By 1810 the confluence once again became a gathering place where these supplies would be handed over to the Indians.

With the outbreak of the War of 1812, the Indians and British would once again join forces to try to keep the country from uniting. During this time, General William Henry Harrison, who fought in the Battle of Fallen Timbers, chose the site for a new fort just south of Fort Defiance. General James Winchester was in charge of building this much larger fort, which was named in his honor. While it was never used for battle, it became a very important supply post during the War of 1812. The Americans won the war and Fort Winchester was abandoned by 1815.

Many American settlers began to move into the rich lands of northwest Ohio. Before their homes could be built, they had to cut down trees and dig ditches to drain the Black Swamp. Fort Winchester served as a first home to many of these families.

TIPPECANOE AND TYLER TOO

Campaign slogan used by Harrison when he ran for President in 1840

Shawnee Chief Tecumseh

General William H. Harrison
Defeated Tecumseh at Tippecanoe

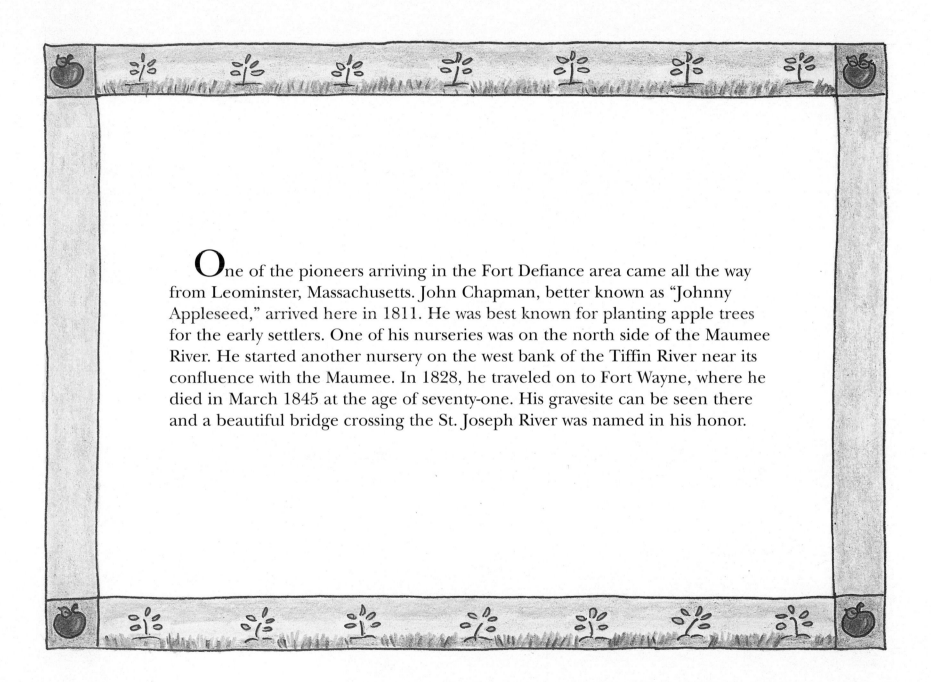

One of the pioneers arriving in the Fort Defiance area came all the way from Leominster, Massachusetts. John Chapman, better known as "Johnny Appleseed," arrived here in 1811. He was best known for planting apple trees for the early settlers. One of his nurseries was on the north side of the Maumee River. He started another nursery on the west bank of the Tiffin River near its confluence with the Maumee. In 1828, he traveled on to Fort Wayne, where he died in March 1845 at the age of seventy-one. His gravesite can be seen there and a beautiful bridge crossing the St. Joseph River was named in his honor.

In 1820 nearly one hundred people lived in the Fort Defiance area. The town was surveyed and the first lot was created in November of 1822. Then on April 23, 1823 the plot was officially recorded. The word "Fort" was dropped from the small town's name and by January of 1836, Defiance was incorporated as a village.

Growth was very slow in Defiance until the building of the canal system. Canals were built in the 1820's to connect many different waterways. The opening of the Ohio-Erie Canal in 1845 linked Lake Erie and the Ohio River. Fortunately for Defiance, part of this system came through the small village, giving the community a better link with the outside world. This waterway was called the Miami-Erie Canal. A Defiance resident could take a boat to Toledo, Ft. Wayne, Dayton or Cincinnati.

SITE
OF
LOCK NO. 13
MIAMI - ERIE
CANAL
BUILT - 1825 - 45

Stone marker - located at
Independence Dam State Park

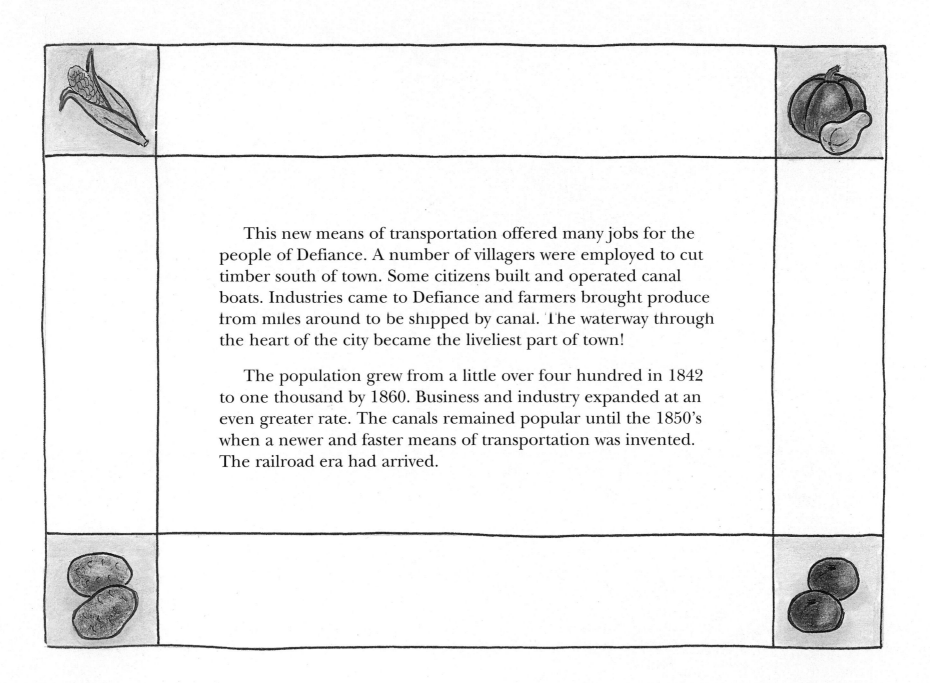

This new means of transportation offered many jobs for the people of Defiance. A number of villagers were employed to cut timber south of town. Some citizens built and operated canal boats. Industries came to Defiance and farmers brought produce from miles around to be shipped by canal. The waterway through the heart of the city became the liveliest part of town!

The population grew from a little over four hundred in 1842 to one thousand by 1860. Business and industry expanded at an even greater rate. The canals remained popular until the 1850's when a newer and faster means of transportation was invented. The railroad era had arrived.

Dr. Charles E. Slocum
1841 - 1915

As the town of Defiance continued to grow in the 1860's, a young man was studying very hard to become a doctor. Charles Elihu Slocum was a student at Columbia University in New York City. He earned his medical degree in 1869 and joined his brother, Dr. John Caleb Slocum in Shelbyville, Indiana.

Shortly after beginning his practice he was forced to take some time off, due to health problems. After traveling through the south, he decided it was time to start practicing medicine again. In 1871, Dr. Charles E. Slocum came to Defiance. He was a very successful doctor, gaining respect from those he served. He continued to study, earning several additional degrees.

Dr. Slocum also had a keen interest in history and published several books. He is well known for his book entitled, *History of the Maumee River Basin.* It covers a wide period of history, including the building of Fort Defiance and the Battle of Fallen Timbers.

He was also the author of *History of Frances Slocum, the Captive.* The story begins in a Quaker settlement along the Susquehanna River in eastern Pennsylvania. Five year old Frances was playing with her brother, when all of a sudden Delaware Indians burst into their home and took her captive! She was taken by canoe to Tioga, an Iroquois village. Frances was then given to a Miami couple that had recently lost a daughter. She was given the name Maconaquah, which means "little bear woman." They traveled westward, settling in a Miami village in Kekionga.

Did Dr. Slocum have a special interest in this very sad, but interesting story? The answer is YES! Dr. Charles Elihu Slocum, physician, historian and writer was a descendent of "little bear woman."

Maconaquah
1773-1847

By 1902 boats operating between Defiance and the state dam would take visitors to Preston Island, located a short distance east of the confluence. Island Park, as it was sometimes called, was named in honor of William Preston, who was thought to be the first permanent white settler at Fort Defiance. The island became a trendy tourist spot in the early 1900's with its wide variety of activities. There was a racetrack, ball park, theater, penny arcade, camp site, and a restaurant, just to name a few. By 1906 there was a streetcar extension from the east side of Hopkins Street to the river.

Preston Island was a very popular place until the Great Flood of 1913. Twenty-three to twenty-six feet of water washed away all of the buildings on the island. Today, set aside as a nature reserve, it is owned by the Black Swamp Chapter of the National Audubon Society.

Anthony Wayne School

Brickell School

The confluence holds within its depths a story rich in history. Native Americans, fur traders, American leaders, soldiers, captives, and settlers are all a very important part of our heritage. Special people are often remembered by naming buildings, parks, and streets in their honor. That is why we have city elementary schools named in honor of General Anthony Wayne, Johnny Brickell, Dr. Charles E. Slocum and Oliver Spencer. Two of our city parks are named for the Native American leaders, Pontiac and Tecumseh. A statue of Chief Little Turtle stands on the campus of Defiance College. Many of our streets are named for United States Presidents, state and community leaders, and important events in history.

Defiance has become the beautiful and productive city that it is today because our leaders have a vision for the future, while at the same time, recognize its unique, historical past. As our community motto states, Defiance truly is "a great place to live!"

Slocum School

Spencer School

Words to Know

Ally — people or countries that work together for a common purpose

Abandon — to give up completely

Archeologist — person who studies ancient cultures through their artifacts

Bison — shaggy, large North American mammal-similar to American buffalo

Campaign — series of operations to reach a planned goal

Confident — sure of oneself

Confluence — a flowing together, as streams

Convoy — protective escort

Council — body of leaders or advisors

Defiance — going against authority

Descendant — offspring of certain ancestor

Expedition — journey for exploration or invasion

Glacier — broad, moving mass of ice

Government — system for running a country

Immigration — entering a country to settle

Independent — free

League — nation

Mega-fauna — huge animal of a particular region or time

Migrate — when people or animals move in a group

Negotiations — working toward making an agreement, as in a treaty

Official — holding a position of authority

Rebel — to go against authority

Relentless — not letting up

Representative — one who acts or speaks for others

Tension — when one feels tense or nervous

Treaty — agreement between two or more nations

Early Timeline of the Confluence and Related Historical Events

1600: Algonquian and Iroquoian Leagues inhabited the area

1600–1650: Fur trading with Europeans

1650–1700: Iroquois Indians from east took over Ohio hunting grounds

1754–1763: French and Indian War

1763: Chief Pontiac organizes allies and attacks British forts

1775: British and American colonists fire at each other in Lexington

1776: Declaration of Independence is signed July 4

1776–1783: American Revolutionary War

1787: Northwest Ordinance is passed

1790: Indian Wars of this area begin

1791: Johnny Brickell is kidnapped by the Indians

1792: Grand council is held at the confluence

1792: President George Washington appoints General Anthony Wayne leader of the U.S. Army

1792: Oliver Spencer is kidnapped by the Indians

1793: General Wayne moves his army across Ohio to the Big Miami River

1794: Over 1,500 warriors come to the confluence ready to fight

1794–December: General Wayne's army builds Fort Recovery

1794-August 2: Fort Adams is built on the St. Marys River, tree falls on General Wayne's tent

1794-August 8: Wayne arrives at the confluence, Fort Defiance built

1794-August 15: Wayne leads army toward present-day Maumee, Ohio

1794: General Wayne wins the famous Battle of Fallen Timbers

1795-August 3: Treaty of Greenville is signed by Indians, Johnny Brickell is set free

1803: Ohio becomes the seventeenth state on March 1

1808: Tecumseh organizes a large band of Shawnee Indians to fight the Americans

1811: John Chapman comes to Fort Defiance, starts a nursery

1812: General William Henry Harrison chooses the site for Fort Winchester, War of 1812 begins

1815: War of 1812 ends

1822-November: town is surveyed and first lot created

1823: Plot is officially recorded

1836: Defiance is incorporated as a village

1845: Opening of the Miami-Erie Canal

1900–1913: Preston Island is a trendy, tourist spot

1913: Great Flood

Index

Illustrations are indicated in bold numbers.

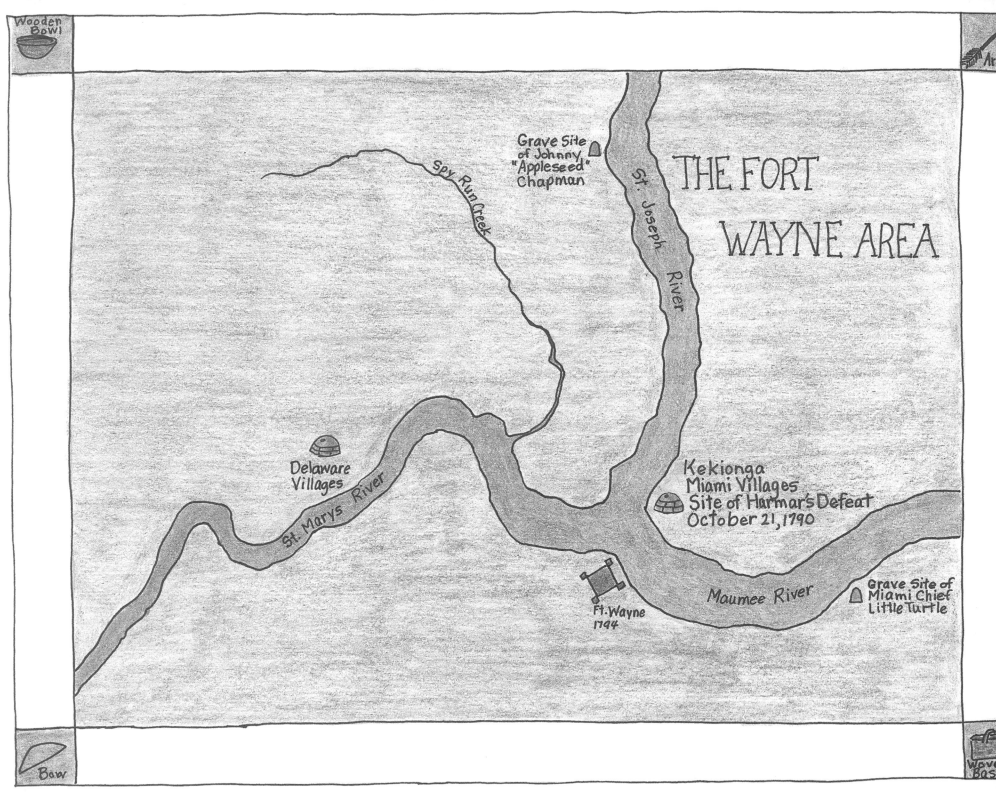